Facts About Countries
The Caribbean

Ian Graham

SEA-TO-SEA
Mankato Collingwood London

This edition first published in 2009 by
Sea-to-Sea Publications
Distributed by Black Rabbit Books
P.O. Box 3263
Mankato, Minnesota 56002

Library of Congress Cataloging-in-Publication Data:

Graham, Ian, 1953-
    The Caribbean / Ian Graham.
        p. cm. -- (Facts about countries)
    Summary: "Describes the geography, history, industries,
education, government, and cultures of the Caribbean Islands,
including Jamaica, the Bahamas, Trinidad and Tobago, and
Barbados. Includes maps, charts, and graphs"--Provided by
publisher.
    Includes index.
    ISBN 978-1-59771-114-2
    1. Caribbean Area--Juvenile literature. I. Title.
    F2161.5.G74 2009
    972.9--dc22
                                2008004633

9 8 7 6 5 4 3 2

Published by arrangement with the Watts Publishing
Group Ltd, London.

Facts About Countries is produced for Franklin
Watts by Bender Richardson White, PO Box 266,
Uxbridge, UK.

Editors: Lionel Bender, Angela Royston
Designer and Page Make-up: Ben White
Picture Researcher: Cathy Stastny
Cover Make-up: Mike Pilley, Radius
Production: Kim Richardson

Graphics and Maps: Stefan Chabluk
Educational Advisor: Prue Goodwin, Institute of
Education, The University of Reading
Consultant: Dr. Terry Jennings, a former geography
teacher and university lecturer. He is now a full-time
writer of children's geography and science books.

Picture Credits

Pages: 1: James Davis Travel Photography. 3: DAS
Photo/David Simson. 4: Hutchison Photo
Library/Philip Wolmuth. 6: DAS Photo/David Simson.
8: Hutchison Photo Library/Brian Moser. 10-11 bottom:
DAS Photo/David Simson. 11: DAS Photo/David
Simson. 12: DAS Photo/David Simson. 13: Hutchison
Photo Library/Errington. 14: DAS Photo/David Simson
15: DAS Photo/David Simson. 16-17: Hutchison Photo
Library/Philip Wolmuth. 18: DAS Photo/David Simson
19: Hutchison Photo Library/Jeremy Horner.
20: DAS Photo/David Simson. 21:DAS Photo/David
Simson. 22: James Davis Travel Photography.
22/23 bottom: Hutchison Photo Library/James
Henderson. 24: Corbis Images Inc/Philip Gould.
25: Corbis Images Inc/Jan Butchofsky. 27: DAS
Photo/David Simson. 29: Hutchison Photo
Library/James Henderson. 30: DAS Photo/David
Simson. 31: DAS Photo/David Simson.
Cover photo: Robert Harding Photo Library.

The Author

Ian Graham is a full-time
writer and editor of non-
fiction books. He has written
more than 100 books for
children.

Note to parents and teachers

Every effort has been made by the Publishers to ensure
that the websites in this book are suitable for children,
that they are of the highest educational value, and that
they contain no inappropriate or offensive material.
However, because of the nature of the Internet, it is
impossible to guarantee that the contents of these sites
will not be altered. We strongly advise that Internet
access is supervised by a responsible adult.

Contents

Welcome to the Caribbean

When people think of the Caribbean, they usually think of white beaches, palm trees, and clear, blue water.

Chains of islands

The Caribbean includes all the islands in the Caribbean Sea. Most of the islands form three chains—the Greater Antilles, the Lesser Antilles, and the Bahamas. The Caribbean also includes Guyana, which is part of South America, and the nearby islands of Trinidad and Tobago.

Below. **Soufrière is a fishing port on St. Lucia. The island is one of the Windward Islands.**

4

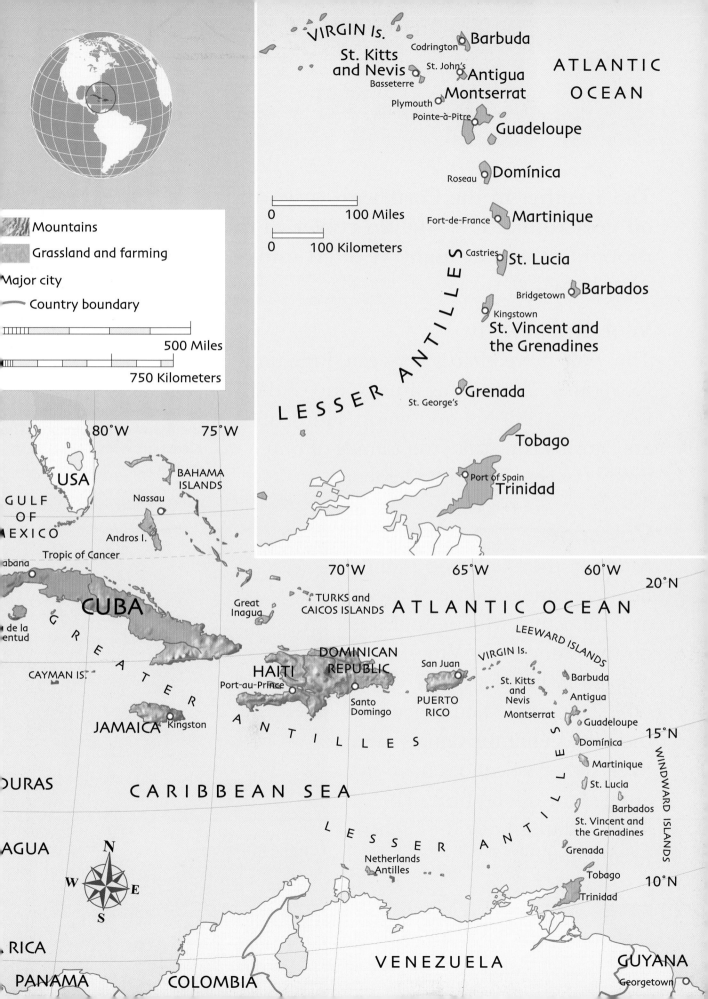

VIRGIN Is.
St. Kitts and Nevis
Barbuda
Codrington
Basseterre
St. John's
Antigua
Montserrat
Plymouth
Pointe-à-Pitre
Guadeloupe
ATLANTIC OCEAN
Roseau
Domínica
Fort-de-France
Martinique
Castries
St. Lucia
Bridgetown
Barbados
Kingstown
St. Vincent and the Grenadines
LESSER ANTILLES
St. George's
Grenada
Tobago
Port of Spain
Trinidad

0   100 Miles
0   100 Kilometers

Mountains
Grassland and farming
Major city
Country boundary

500 Miles
750 Kilometers

80°W   75°W
USA
BAHAMA ISLANDS
GULF OF MEXICO
Nassau
Andros I.
Tropic of Cancer
abana
CUBA
de la entud
CAYMAN IS.
GREATER
Great Inagua
TURKS and CAICOS ISLANDS
ATLANTIC OCEAN
70°W   65°W   60°W   20°N
DOMINICAN REPUBLIC
HAITI
Port-au-Prince
San Juan
VIRGIN Is.
LEEWARD ISLANDS
St. Kitts and Nevis
Barbuda
Antigua
Montserrat
Guadeloupe
JAMAICA
Kingston
ANTILLES
Santo Domingo
PUERTO RICO
Domínica
15°N
Martinique
St. Lucia
CARIBBEAN SEA
Barbados
St. Vincent and the Grenadines
WINDWARD ISLANDS
DURAS
LESSER
ANTILLES
Grenada
AGUA
Netherlands Antilles
Tobago
10°N
Trinidad
N
W   E
S
RICA
VENEZUELA
GUYANA
PANAMA
COLOMBIA
Georgetown

The Land

The weather in the Caribbean is warm all year round. It is slightly cooler in the mountains and at night. It often rains very heavily.

Wet and stormy

The wettest weather is between June and November. During this time, some of the islands are very hot and damp. Hurricanes and storms can strike the islands at any time between July and October.

All the Caribbean islands have lizards, snakes, and colorful birds, especially parrots. Only Trinidad has monkeys and other mammals. The sea is filled with life, too. Coral reefs are home to more than 1,000 kinds of fish.

Below. Coconut palms and many other plants grow on the island of St. Vincent. The plants grow well because it rains a lot.

Volcanoes

Many of the Caribbean islands have volcanoes. Some of these are still active. Mount Soufrière on the island of St. Vincent erupted in 1812, 1902, 1971, and 1979. The people had to leave the island until the danger was over. Other volcanoes have not erupted for a long time. The largest islands have the highest mountains.

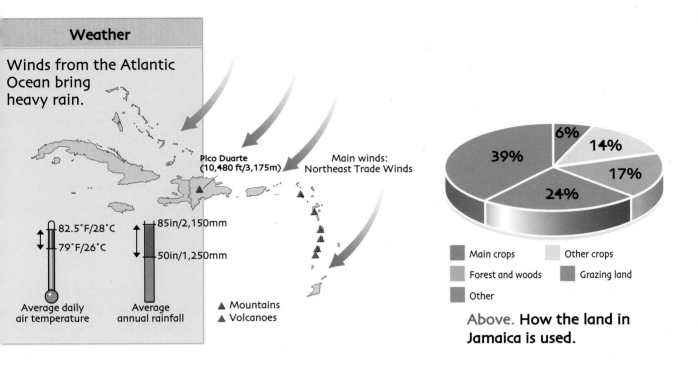

Weather

Winds from the Atlantic Ocean bring heavy rain.

Pico Duarte
(10,480 ft/3,175m)

Main winds:
Northeast Trade Winds

82.5°F/28°C
79°F/26°C

Average daily air temperature

85in/2,150mm
50in/1,250mm

Average annual rainfall

▲ Mountains
▲ Volcanoes

6%
14%
17%
24%
39%

■ Main crops   ■ Other crops
■ Forest and woods   ■ Grazing land
■ Other

Above. How the land in Jamaica is used.

Below. Average rainfall each month in Kingston, Jamaica.

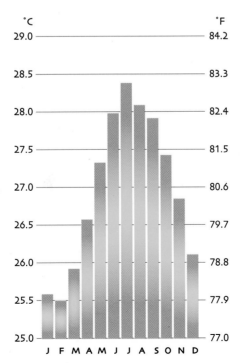

mm | in
8
7
6
5
4
3
2
1
0

J F M A M J J A S O N D

Below. Average temperatures in Kingston, Jamaica.

°C | °F
29.0 — 84.2
28.5 — 83.3
28.0 — 82.4
27.5 — 81.5
27.0 — 80.6
26.5 — 79.7
26.0 — 78.8
25.5 — 77.9
25.0 — 77.0

J F M A M J J A S O N D

Web Search ▶▶

▶ www.barbados.org/
   weather.htm
   The weather and climate in Barbados.

▶ www.caribwx.com/climate1.
   html
   The weather in British Virgin Islands.

▶ www.worldclimate.com
   Facts and figures on world climate.

The People

Origins

There are 36 million people living in the Caribbean today. Their ancestors came from all over the world.

Slave trading

Most Caribbeans have ancestors from West Africa. They were brought to the islands by European slave traders 300 to 400 years ago. The slaves worked on sugar plantations.

The Caribbean is named after the Carib Indians. They were living in the Lesser Antilles when the first Spanish explorers invaded and took over the islands in the fifteenth century.

Below. Caribbeans shop at a street market on Curaçao, an island in the Lesser Antilles.

Asian ancestors

More people arrived in the Caribbean between 100 and 200 years ago. They came from India and China. Many of them still speak Hindi, Urdu, and Chinese.

Main languages

Many Caribbeans speak Spanish, English, French, or Dutch. These are the languages of the Europeans who colonized the islands. The slaves developed their own languages—pidgin and creole. Some Caribbean languages are made up of many languages.

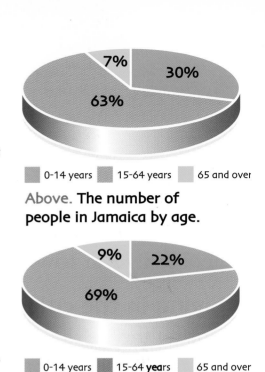

Above. **The number of people in Jamaica by age.**

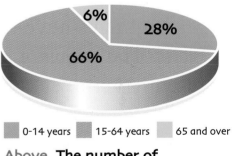

Above. **The number of people in Barbados by age.**

Above. **The number of people in Trinidad and Tobago by age.**

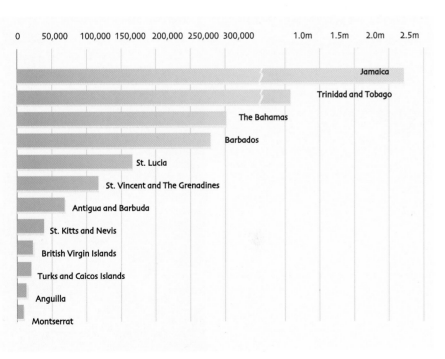

Above. **The number of people who live on some of the islands in the Caribbean.**

Web Search ►►

► www.avirtualdominica.com/
caribs.htm
Facts about Carib Indians on
the island of Dominica.

► www.usaid.gov/locations/
latin_america_caribbean/
The ways the U.S. aids the
Caribbean people.

Town and Country Life

At one time, most people in the Caribbean worked on farms in the countryside. Now, more than half of its people live in towns and cities.

Living in the cities

During the last 100 years, many people left the countryside to find work in the towns and cities. Towns on the coast have become popular places for tourists on vacation. Shantytowns have grown up around the cities. The people who live in shantytowns often have no electricity or clean water.

Kingston, Jamaica

More than 500,000 people live in Kingston, the capital of Jamaica. Another 200,000 more people live in the suburbs around Kingston.

Jamaica became a British colony in 1655.

Kingston was founded in 1692. Its name means "king's town" in honor of the British king at the time, William III.

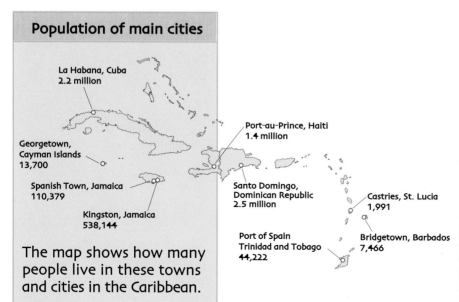

Population of main cities

La Habana, Cuba
2.2 million

Georgetown,
Cayman Islands
13,700

Spanish Town, Jamaica
110,379

Kingston, Jamaica
538,144

Port-au-Prince, Haiti
1.4 million

Santo Domingo,
Dominican Republic
2.5 million

Castries, St. Lucia
1,991

Port of Spain
Trinidad and Tobago
44,222

Bridgetown, Barbados
7,466

The map shows how many people live in these towns and cities in the Caribbean.

Left. This wooden shanty is in Sandy Bay, in Jamaica. More than one-third of Jamaicans are poor.

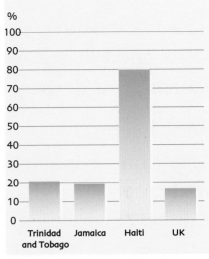

Above. Comparing the percentage of poor people in three Caribbean countries and in the United Kingdom.

Street Markets

People meet at the street markets. There people sell fruit and vegetables they have grown on their plots of land. This includes yams, plantains, bananas, and squashes.

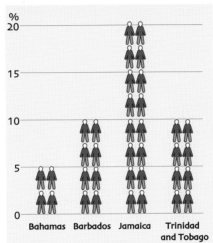

Above. The percentages of people who work in farming in four Caribbean countries.

Left. Nassau, the capital of the Bahamas. Most towns and cities in the Caribbean grew larger and richer when they became tourist resorts.

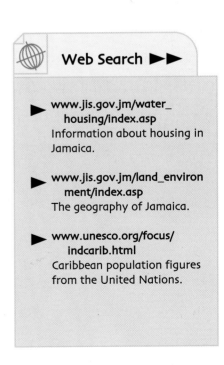

Web Search ►►

► www.jis.gov.jm/water_ housing/index.asp
Information about housing in Jamaica.

► www.jis.gov.jm/land_environ ment/index.asp
The geography of Jamaica.

► www.unesco.org/focus/ indcarib.html
Caribbean population figures from the United Nations.

Farming and Fishing

The Caribbean's warm, wet weather is very good for growing crops. But its storms can destroy the crops in minutes.

Main crops

Sugarcane, bananas, coffee beans, tobacco, and cocoa are the main crops grown in the Caribbean. They are grown on plantations, and are sold all over the world. People who live in the countryside also grow other plants and keep animals on their plots of land.

Fishing

The Caribbean Sea is full of fish, but most of them are small and swim around coral reefs. Fishermen catch large amounts of fish in only a few places.

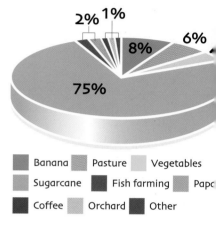

2% 1%
6%
8%
75%

Banana	Pasture	Vegetables
Sugarcane	Fish farming	Papo
Coffee	Orchard	Other

Above. **Areas of land and lakes used for different kinds of farming.**

Making pure sugar

1. Crush stalks of sugarcane to make sap.
2. Leave sap in tanks to clear.
3. Boil sap to make a thick syrup.
4. Dry syrup to make brown sugar.
5. Refine brown sugar to get white sugar.

Left. **This plantation on St. Lucia grows thousands of tons of bananas each year.**

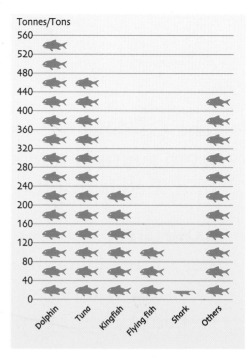

Tonnes/Tons

Above. Weights of different kinds of fish caught by boats from St. Lucia.

Above. A fisherman near the coast of Grenada holds up a puffer fish that was trapped in his net. This fish will be returned to the sea.

Farming and Fishing

Large amounts of fish are mostly caught around the Bahamas.

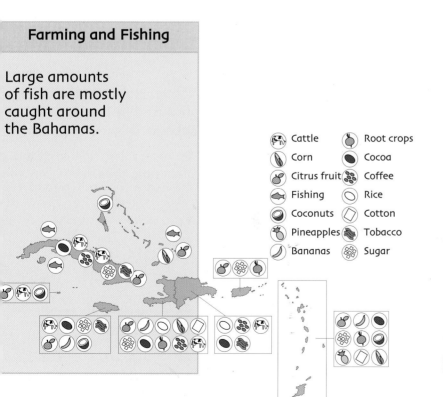

Cattle
Corn
Citrus fruit
Fishing
Coconuts
Pineapples
Bananas
Root crops
Cocoa
Coffee
Rice
Cotton
Tobacco
Sugar

Web Search ▶▶

▶ www.cbea.org
The Caribbean Banana Exporters Association.

▶ www.jamaica-gleaner.com/pages/history/story0029.html
History of Jamaica's coffee .

▶ www.caricom–fisheries.com/
Fishing industry of many Caribbean countries.

Resources and Industry

The Caribbean makes most of its money from tourism and selling its crops, oil, and metals to other countries.

Tourism

For some islands, tourism is the main industry. Tourists enjoy the beaches, the scenery, and the hot, sunny weather.

Above. Bauxite is rich in aluminum. Jamaica mines and produces more than 12,000 tons of bauxite a year.

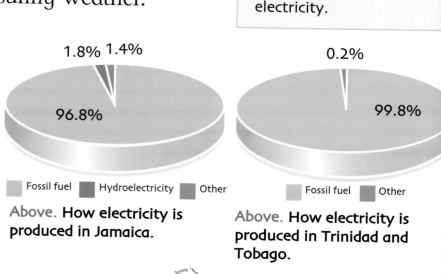

1.8% 1.4%

96.8%

Fossil fuel   Hydroelectricity   Other

Above. **How electricity is produced in Jamaica.**

0.2%

99.8%

Fossil fuel   Other

Above. **How electricity is produced in Trinidad and Tobago.**

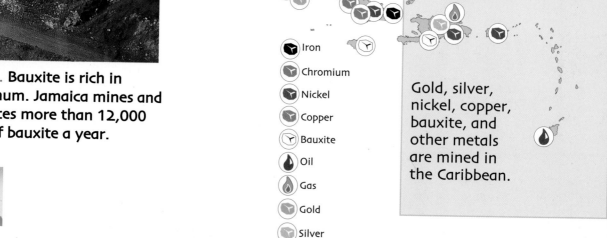

- Iron
- Chromium
- Nickel
- Copper
- Bauxite
- Oil
- Gas
- Gold
- Silver

Resources and Industry

Gold, silver, nickel, copper, bauxite, and other metals are mined in the Caribbean.

Sugar trade

Europeans set up large plantations to grow sugarcane on many of the islands in the Caribbean. Some sugar is made into rum, an alcoholic drink. Most of the sugar and rum are sold to European countries.

Other industries

Caribbean countries also make clothes and furniture, and mine metals. The Bahamas and Trinidad and Tobago have oil wells. Some of the oil is made into different kinds of plastic.

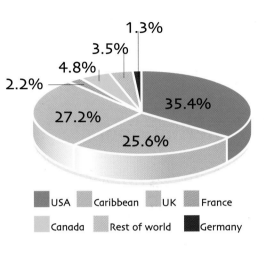

1.3%
3.5%
4.8%
2.2%
35.4%
27.2%
25.6%

USA Caribbean UK France
Canada Rest of world Germany

Above. **Where tourists visiting St. Lucia come from.**

Below. **The Caribbean's tropical climate makes it popular with tourists. Many sail from island to island on huge, expensive cruise ships.**

Web Search ►►

► **www.gov.tt**
Trinidad and Tobago government information.

► **www.stats.gov.lc**
St. Lucia government facts and figures.

► **www.caribbeantravel.com/**
Tourism in the Caribbean.

Transportation

It is easy to travel to and around the Caribbean. Most islands have an airport and good harbors for yachts and ferries. There are also docks for international cargo ships.

Planes

Most islands have international airports with flights to Europe, the U.S., and Canada. Island-hoppers are small planes that fly between the islands from small airports.

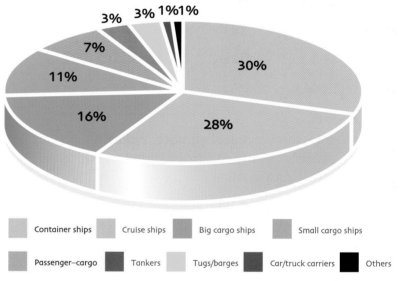

Container ships	Cruise ships	Big cargo ships	Small cargo ships
Passenger–cargo	Tankers	Tugs/barges	Car/truck carriers	Others

Above. The kinds of ships that sail to St. Lucia each year.

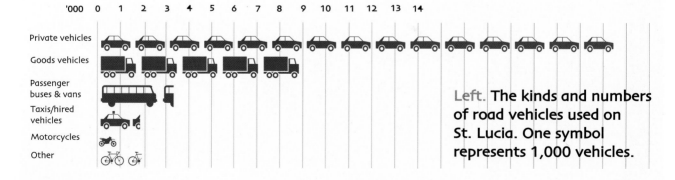

Left. The kinds and numbers of road vehicles used on St. Lucia. One symbol represents 1,000 vehicles.

Left. Passengers board a small plane at Canefield Airport, Dominica.

Road Traffic

On islands that were colonized by Britain, vehicles drive on the left side of the road, as they do in Britain. These islands include Jamaica, Barbados, Trinidad and Tobago, and the British Virgin Islands. On the islands colonized by other European countries, vehicles drive on the right side of the road.

Road and rail

Towns and cities have modern, paved roads. In the countryside, many roads are dirt tracks. Most islands have buses and taxis. A few islands have railroads, too. They are used mainly by the sugar plantations and mines.

Transportation

The main airports and sea routes in the Caribbean.

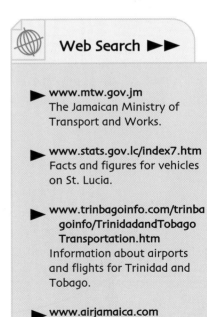

⊗ International airports

  Shipping lanes

Web Search ►►

► www.mtw.gov.jm
  The Jamaican Ministry of Transport and Works.

► www.stats.gov.lc/index7.htm
  Facts and figures for vehicles on St. Lucia.

► www.trinbagoinfo.com/trinba
  goinfo/TrinidadandTobago
  Transportation.htm
  Information about airports and flights for Trinidad and Tobago.

► www.airjamaica.com
  The website of Air Jamaica.

Education

Most schools in the Caribbean are free and are run by the government. The larger islands have a few private schools, which charge fees to parents.

Primary school

Children start school when they are four or five years old. On some Caribbean islands, school starts at 7:30 A.M. and finishes at 2 P.M.

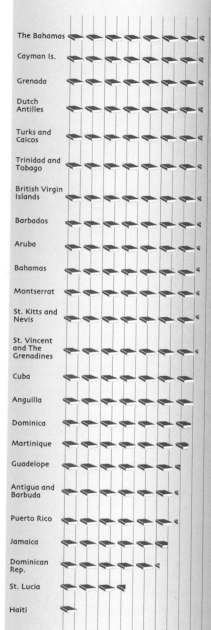

The Bahamas
Cayman Is.
Grenada
Dutch Antilles
Turks and Caicos
Trinidad and Tobago
British Virgin Islands
Barbados
Aruba
Bahamas
Montserrat
St. Kitts and Nevis
St. Vincent and The Grenadines
Cuba
Anguilla
Dominica
Martinique
Guadelope
Antigua and Barbuda
Puerto Rico
Jamaica
Dominican Rep.
St. Lucia
Haiti

Above. The percentages of people on some of the islands who can read.

Left. A secondary-school student in Barbados looks through a microscope during a science lesson.

18

Secondary school

Children go to secondary school when they are 11 years old. There they study languages, math, science, art, and other subjects. When they are 16, students take the Caribbean Examination Council (CXC) exams. At age 18 they may take the Advanced Level exams.

University

The main university is the University of the West Indies. It is based mainly in Jamaica, Barbados, and Trinidad, but there are smaller branches on other islands, too.

Above. **Pupils at a primary school in St. Lucia. Most school children in the Caribbean wear a uniform.**

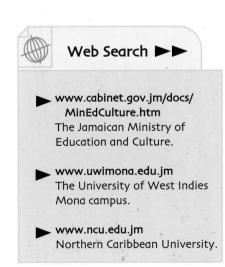

Web Search ►►

► www.cabinet.gov.jm/docs/
MinEdCulture.htm
The Jamaican Ministry of Education and Culture.

► www.uwimona.edu.jm
The University of West Indies Mona campus.

► www.ncu.edu.jm
Northern Caribbean University.

Sports and Leisure

Caribbean sportsmen and sportswomen are among the best in the world. The Jamaican netball team is becoming as famous as the West Indies' cricket team. Soccer is popular, too.

Olympic Games

Caribbean athletes take part in many events. In spite of the Caribbean's warm climate, the Jamaican bobsled team competed in three Winter Olympic Games.

Test Cricket

International cricket matches are known as test matches. Between 1970 and 1980, the West Indies cricket team was the best in the world. It lost only two of the test matches that it played.

Below. **Horseracing at Bridgetown in Barbados.**

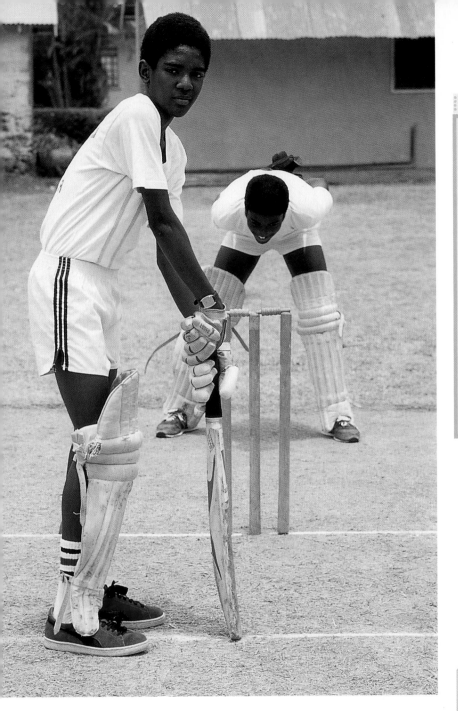

Left. Many children like to play cricket. Here, one boy gets ready to bat. The other boy is the wicketkeeper.

Web Search ►►

► www.top5jamaica.com/category/Sport/
All about Jamaican sports.

► www.westindies.cricinfo.com
Cricket in the West Indies.

► www.jamaicans.com/bobsled/
The Jamaican bobsled team.

Leisure

Tourists and local people enjoy many sports and activities. Water sports include diving, snorkeling, windsurfing, parasailing, and swimming. People also hike, and go rock climbing and horse riding.

Daily Life and Religion

Everyday life in the Caribbean is busy and noisy, especially in the towns and cities. Religion is important to many Caribbean people.

Daily life

Life varies from island to island and between the city and the countryside. Each day, people shop for food, usually in markets.

DATABASE

Medical services

Healthcare varies in the Caribbean but is generally good. The number of babies that die soon after birth measures how good the medical services are. In Barbados, nine babies die out of every 1,000 born. In Haiti, 100 die out of every 1,000.

Left. **This fruit market is in St. George's, the capital of Grenada.**

22

European religions

Most Caribbean people are Christian. On islands colonized by Spain and France, many people are Catholic. On islands colonized by Britain, most people are Protestant.

Other religions

Many people, especially in Trinidad, are Hindu or Muslim. Rastafarianism is a religion popular in Jamaica. It praises the Ethiopian emperor, Haile Selassie. Voodoo mixes Roman Catholic and African beliefs.

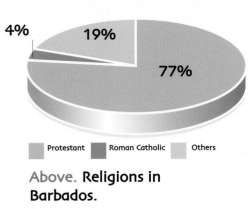

Above. **Religions in Barbados.**

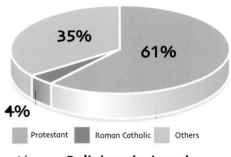

Above. **Religions in Jamaica.**

Below. **Protestants hold services every Sunday in this parish church in Mandeville, in Jamaica.**

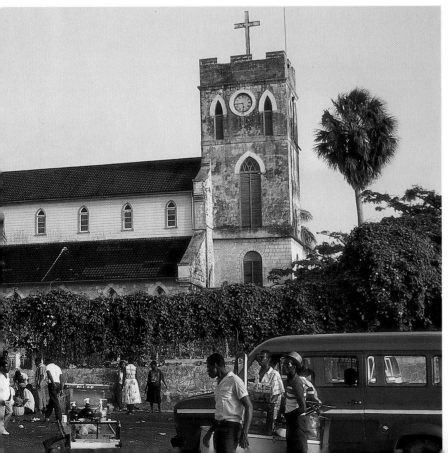

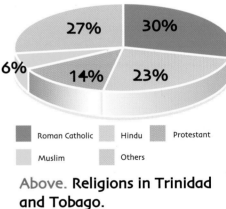

Above. **Religions in Trinidad and Tobago.**

Web Search ▶▶

▶ www.barbados.org/churches.htm
Information on the different churches in Barbados.

▶ www.moh.gov.jm/
The Jamaican Ministry of Health.

Arts and Media

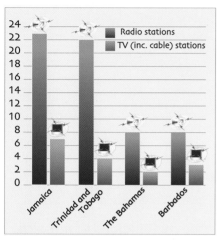

Above. **The number of radio and television stations on four Caribbean islands or island groups.**

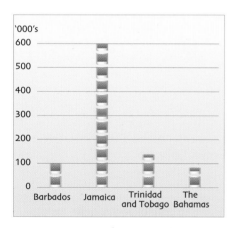

Above. **The number of people on these Caribbean islands who own televisions and radios.**

Right. **Carnival time in Martinique. People dress up and dance in the streets.**

Music and dance are a big part of Caribbean culture. Many Caribbean writers are well known and respected all over the world.

Music

Reggae, calypso, and steel band music all began in the Caribbean. The music is based on rhythms, melodies, and stories that the slaves brought with them from Africa. Steel bands began in Trinidad in the 1930s. The top of a drum is hammered into shapes that each make a different sound when they are hit with a drumstick.

Above. **Steel bands are popular all year round on many islands in the Caribbean.**

Famous Caribbean Writers

V.S. Naipaul (born in Trinidad in 1932) has written several novels set in the Caribbean.

Derek Walcott (born in St. Lucia in 1930) won the Nobel Prize for Literature in 1992. He writes poetry and plays.

Samuel Selvon (1923-94) wrote about the lives and experiences of Indian immigrants to the Caribbean.

Andrew Salkey (1928-95) wrote plays, novels, and poems about Jamaica.

Newspapers

Most islands have their own newspapers. Newspapers in most Caribbean countries are free to criticize the government.

Radio and television

Some television and radio stations are owned by the government. Others are privately owned. People can watch satellite and cable television from the United States.

Web Search ▶▶

▶ www.sbgmusic.com/html/ teacher/reference/cultures/ jamaica.html
The development of Jamaican song and dance.

▶ www.jamaicaobserver.com
Website of the *Jamaica Observer* newspaper.

▶ www.guardian.co.tt
Trinidad Guardian newspaper.

▶ www.thenassauguardian.com
Nassau Guardian newspaper, Bahamas.

25

Government

Most countries in the Caribbean are ruled by governments that the people vote for every few years.

Independence

During the 1960s and 1970s, most Caribbean countries became independent. This means that they were no longer ruled by the European countries that had colonized them. However, many countries still keep close links with their former rulers.

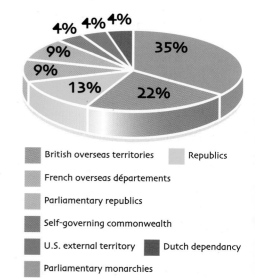

- British overseas territories
- French overseas départements
- Parliamentary republics
- Self-governing commonwealth
- U.S. external territory
- Parliamentary monarchies
- Republics
- Dutch dependancy

Above. Different kinds of government in the Caribbean.

Invasion

In Grenada in 1979, the army overthrew the country's government. In 1983, a military force led by the United States invaded the island. The people of Grenada then elected a new government.

Right. **The type of government in different countries in the Caribbean.**

Government status of some Caribbean countries

Country	Status	Since
Antigua and Barbuda	Parliamentary monarchy	1981
Bahamas	Parliamentary monarchy	1973
Barbados	Parliamentary monarchy	1966
British Virgin Islands	British overseas territory	1960
Cuba	Republic	1898
Dominican Republic	Republic	1865
Grenada	Parliamentary monarchy	1974
Guadeloupe	French overseas département	1946
Guyana	Parliamentary republic	1966
Haiti	Republic	1804
Jamaica	Parliamentary monarchy	1962
Montserrat	British overseas territory	1960
Puerto Rico	Self-governing commonwealth	1952
St. Kitts and Nevis	Parliamentary monarchy	1983
St. Lucia	Parliamentary monarchy	1979
Trinidad and Tobago	Parliamentary republic	1962
Turks and Caicos Islands	British overseas territory	1972
U.S. Virgin Islands	U.S. external territory	1917

A monarchy has a king or queen as head of state.
A republic is led by a president—if there is a royal family, it has no power.
A département or an external or overseas territory is still partly governed by the original ruling country.

Kinds of government

Many countries that were once British colonies became parliamentary monarchies. This means they elect their own parliament but have the British monarch as their head of state. Parliamentary republics elect their own parliament, too, but elect a president as head of state. Some countries are British Overseas Territories. They elect their own government, but they have a governor who is appointed by Britain.

Below. **A soldier stands on guard outside the government offices in Nassau in the Bahamas.**

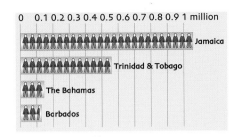

Above. **The number of workers in some of the main Caribbean countries.**

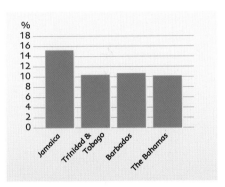

Above. **Workers in these islands who do not have work.**

Web Search ▶▶

▶ www.gov.tt
The government of Trinidad and Tobago.

▶ www.stlucia.gov.lc
The government of St. Lucia.

▶ www.caribinfo.com/govern ment.html
Information about all the Caribbean governments.

Place in the World

Historical Events until the 1970s

1000
Carib Indians settle in the Windward Islands

1498
Christopher Columbus reaches Trinidad

1510
Spain occupies Jamaica

1620s
St. Kitts becomes Britain's first Caribbean colony

1627
British colonists arrive on Barbados

1637
Sugarcane first grown in Barbados

1655
Britain takes Jamaica from Spain

1834
Slavery abolished in British Caribbean

1960s
Many islands gain independence

1968
Caribbean Free Trade Association (CARIFTA) is formed

Caribbean countries are members of many international organizations. They also trade with each other and with the rest of the world.

International organizations

Countries in the Caribbean belong to many organizations, including the United Nations (UN) and the International Olympic Committee. Many Caribbean countries joined an organization for former British colonies called the Commonwealth.

Below. **The flags of some of the main Caribbean countries.**

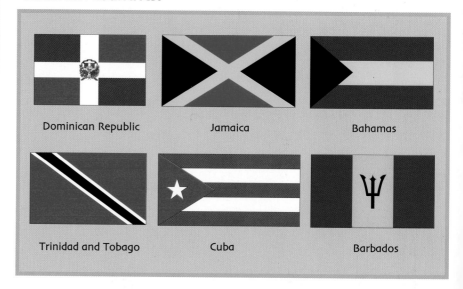

Dominican Republic   Jamaica   Bahamas

Trinidad and Tobago   Cuba   Barbados

Above. The Palais de Justice (Law Courts) at Port de France on Martinique. People in Martinique and Guadeloupe have to obey French laws and elect representatives to the French parliament in Paris.

Trade

The Caribbean Community and Common Market (CARICOM) is an organization that helps Caribbean countries trade with one another. Most international trade used to be with the European countries that colonized the Caribbean. Now, most international trade is with the United States.

Below. Total money earned on some Caribbean islands.

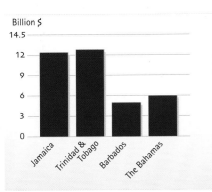

Below. Money earned from exports from some Caribbean islands.

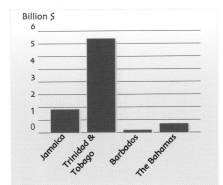

DATABASE

Historical Events since the 1970s

1970s
Many other islands gain independence

1981
The Organization of Eastern Caribbean States formed

1982
Anguilla becomes a British Dependent Territory

1983
St. Kitts and Nevis gains independence

1997
Volcanic eruptions on Montserrat destroy town of Plymouth

2000
More volcanic eruptions on Montserrat

 Web Search ►►

► www.oecs.org
The Organization of Eastern Caribbean States.

► www.jftc.com
Jamaica Fair Trading Commission.

► www.caricom.org
Caribbean Community and Common Market.

These figures are for Jamaica, the Bahamas, Barbados, and Trinidad and Tobago.

Total area: 11,7770 sq miles (30,488 sq km)

Total population: 4,397,734

Capital cities:
Kingston, Jamaica (population 538,144)
Nassau, Bahamas (172,196)
Bridgetown, Barbados (96,758)
Port-of-Spain, Trinidad and Tobago (44,222)

Longest river:
Black River, Jamaica (44 miles/71 km)

Highest mountain:
Blue Mountain Peak, Jamaica (7,400ft/2,256 m)

Jamaica's flag:
A gold diagonal cross with two black and two green triangles. Gold is for the island's natural wealth and sunlight; green, hope and farming resources; the black, hardships overcome.

Official language:
English

Currencies:
Jamaican dollar (J$), Bahamian dollar (B$), Barbadian dollar (Bds$), Trinidad and Tobago dollar (TT$)

Major resources:
Bauxite, gypsum, limestone, natural gas, petroleum, asphalt, salt, timber

Major exports:
Bauxite, sugar, rum, alumina, bananas, coffee, cocoa, cement

Some public holidays:
January 1: New Year's Day
Mid-February to early March: Carnival, Trinidad and Tobago
Late March to late April: Good Friday, Easter Monday

May 1: Labor Day, Barbados
May 23: Labor Day, Jamaica
1st Friday in June: Labor Day, Bahamas
June 19: Labor Day, Trinidad and Tobago
July 10: Independence Day, Bahamas
1st Monday in August: Independence Day, Jamaica
August 31: Independence Day, Trinidad and Tobago
October 16: National Heroes' Day, Jamaica
November 30: Independence Day, Barbados
December 25: Christmas Day

Main religions:
Protestantism, Roman Catholicism, Hinduism, Islam, Rastafarianism, Voodoo

Key Words

ANCESTOR
A grandparent or other relative from whom you are descended.

CARGO
Goods or products carried in a ship, airplane, or truck.

CLIMATE
The kind of weather a place usually has at different times of the year.

COLONY
A country ruled by another country.

EXPORTS
Goods sold to a foreign country.

FOSSIL FUEL
A fuel such as coal, oil, or natural gas that has formed from the bodies of plants and animals that died millions of years ago.

GOVERNMENT
The organization that runs a country.

HURRICANE
A powerful, destructive storm; hurricane-force winds exceeding 99mph (160 km/h).

IMMIGRANTS
People coming to live and work in a country from other countries.

INDEPENDENT
Ruled by people living in the country and not by another country.

MEDICAL SERVICES
Hospitals, doctors, and organizations that keep people healthy and look after sick people.

PARLIAMENT
A group of people elected to represent the people and make new laws in a country.

PLANTATION
An area of farmland on which trees or shrubs are grown for their fruit or leaves.

REPUBLIC
A form of government, usually led by a president, in which people are elected to hold power.

RESOURCES
The raw materials, land, and people's skills that a country uses to make money.

SHANTY
A house made out of waste material.

TOURISM
The industry of vacationers, hotels, and beach resorts.

TRADE
Buying and selling goods.

TROPICAL
The part of the Earth that lies on each side of the Equator; tropical can also mean very warm or hot and damp, like the climate in the tropics.

Index